RAIN FOREST
REPTILES AND AMPHIBIANS

Text and Photography by Edward Parker

RAINTREE
STECK-VAUGHN
PUBLISHERS

A Harcourt Company

Austin   New York
www.raintreesteckvaughn.com

Published by Raintree Steck-Vaughn Publishers,
an imprint of Steck-Vaughn Company

Library of Congress Cataloging-in-Publication data is available upon request.

ISBN 0-7398-5243-4

Printed in Hong Kong. Bound in the United States.

1 2 3 4 5 6 7 8 9 0 LB 07 06 05 04 03 02

Editor: Sarah Doughty
Design: Bernard Higton
Text consultant: Dr. Paul Toyne

Picture acknowledgments:
All photographs are by Edward Parker with the exception of the following: Ecoscene 43 (W. Lawler); OSF 8 (Zig Leszczynski), 9 top (Michael Fogden), 15 top (Robert A. Lubeck/Animals/ Animals), 15 bottom (J.A.L Cooke), 18 both (David M. Dennis), 26 bottom (Michael Fogden), 31 top (Joe McDonald Animals/ Animals), 32 top (Mike Linley/Survival Anglia), 40 (Paul Franklin); Papilio 14 bottom (Paul Franklin).

CONTENTS

① Welcome to the Rain Forest 4

② Diversity 12

③ Home and Habitat 20

④ Survival in the Rain Forest 24

⑤ Disappearing Species 32

⑥ Conservation 38

⑦ The Future 44

Glossary 46

Further Information 47

Index 48

The Rain Forest Home

Reptiles and amphibians are cold-blooded creatures that live both on land and in water. They can live in almost all regions on Earth, but are well suited to the warmth and dampness of the tropics. Rain forests are found near the equator, between the tropics of Cancer and Capricorn. Temperatures are high and rainfall is greater than 79 inches (2,000 mm) every year. Rain forests are found in parts of South and Central America, Africa, Southeast Asia, and Australia. The rain forests are home to some of the world's most interesting and unusual reptiles and amphibians.

▼ A map showing the extent of the world's tropical rain forests today, compared with five hundred years ago, before large-scale deforestation began.

▶ The warm, moist conditions found in rain forests provide amphibians, such as this banana frog, with ideal living conditions.

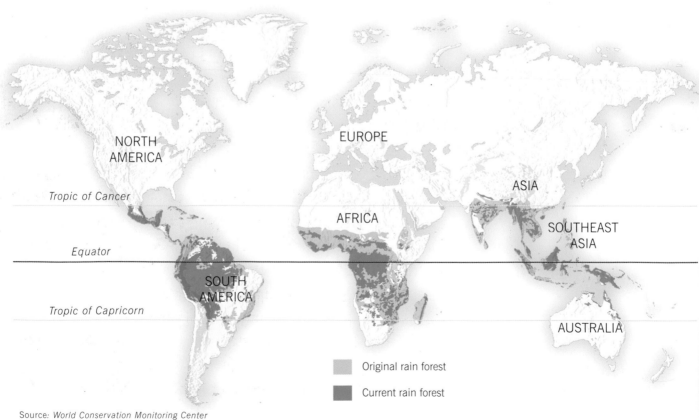

NORTH AMERICA

EUROPE

ASIA

AFRICA

SOUTHEAST ASIA

Tropic of Cancer

Equator

SOUTH AMERICA

Tropic of Capricorn

AUSTRALIA

◻ Original rain forest

◼ Current rain forest

Source: *World Conservation Monitoring Center*

Snakes are reptiles that slither through the vegetation. This red-tailed racer from Southeast Asia is typical of snakes commonly found in the world's rain forests.

Reptiles and Amphibians of the Amazon Rain Forest

The Amazon region of South America is the largest area of continuous rain forest on Earth. In the Amazon, giant snakes up to 30 feet (9 m) long swim in the rivers and slither between tall trees in search of prey. In the twilight world of the rain forest floor, brilliantly colored poison-arrow frogs hop through the dead leaves that gather at the base of trees. High above the forest floor, cup-shaped plants called bromeliads collect water and provide homes for tadpoles and young frogs. Along the edges of rivers and in shallow lakes, huge caimans float like harmless logs before striking their prey with lightning speed.

This book will focus mainly on the reptiles and amphibians that live in the Amazon rain forest. Like all rain forests, the Amazon has special types of reptile and amphibian that do not exist anywhere else in the world.

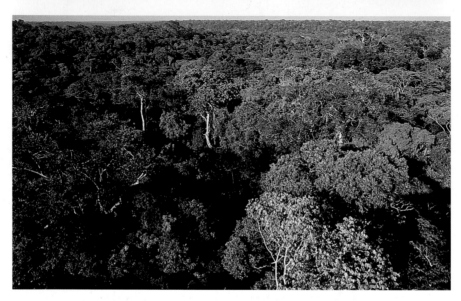

There are many species of amphibian and reptile that have evolved to live in the cooler conditions of the tropical montane forests.

Lowland forests are home to thousands of species of amphibian and reptile.

Types of Rain Forest

Tropical rain forests can be divided into two main types, according to their height above sea level. These are lowland forest and tropical montane forest. Lowland forests are the most widespread and contain the majority of reptiles and amphibians. Tropical montane forest occurs on hills and mountains above 3,000 feet (900 m), where conditions are generally cooler. The trees in tropical montane forests are typically shorter than those in lowland forests and are often hidden in dense mists, which is why montane forests are also called "cloud forests." Tropical montane forests are home to their own species of reptile and amphibian, such as the smoky mountain frog that lives in Central America.

Fascinating Fact

Some species of frog in Madagascar are adapting to other habitats as their natural home is lost through deforestation.

THE SPECTACLED CAIMAN

Caimans are found in Central and South America. Their habitat ranges from southern Mexico to Brazil. The spectacled caiman (see right) is recognized by the bony ridge between its eyes, which is like the nosepiece on a pair of glasses. It is the most common species of caiman—more common than the yellow caiman or the black caiman, which both share the same habitat.

All caimans feed on fish. They also eat deer and tapirs and sometimes birds. Occasionally they will eat other caimans. They are fearsome predators and at the top of the food chain. They hunt by stealth, often lying completely still below the surface of the water with just their eyes and nostrils visible, waiting to take their prey by surprise.

Spectacled caimans have bony deposits on their bodies, rather like armor plating. This makes their skins difficult to sell. For this reason spectacled caimans have not been hunted as heavily as the black and yellow species which share the same habitats.

The Importance of Reptiles and Amphibians

Reptiles and amphibians play an important part in the rain forest ecosystem. The role of frogs, for example, is vital in the rain forest food chain because they eat insects. In this way frogs control the number of insects, but they also provide a source of food for fish, mammals, reptiles, birds, and spiders. Snakes and lizards are the main source of food for some species of bird, like the snake-eating eagle, and mammals such as the mongoose. The eggs of turtles are also an important source of food for mammals and birds, as are the young soft-shelled hatchlings. Caimans control the number of piranhas in Amazonian rivers, but small species of caiman also provide occasional food for the world's largest snake, the anaconda.

What Is an Amphibian?

An amphibian is a partly aquatic animal, such as a frog, toad, salamander, or newt. The word "amphibian" comes from the Latin words "amphi" and "bios," meaning "double life." This refers to the way amphibians spend the first part of their lives in water and their adult lives on dry land. Almost all amphibians follow this sequence. Frogs, for example, begin life as larvae (tadpoles) after hatching underwater from soft eggs, and breathe through their gills. As they grow, they start to change from tadpoles into miniature frogs. After a few weeks, their tail disappears, four legs grow, and lungs develop to replace their gills. When they are fully grown, amphibians live on dry land but will often enter the water, mainly to breed. Amphibians gain and lose water through their skin, so they must keep themselves moist.

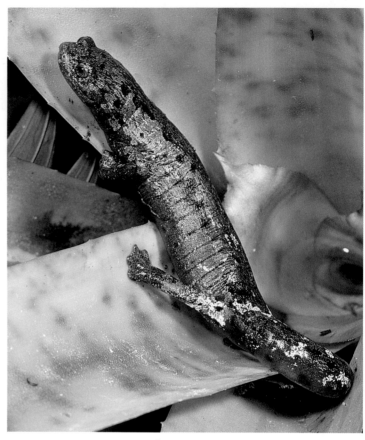

▲ Salamanders, like this bromeliad salamander from Guatemala, are one of four main types of rain forest amphibian.

What Is a Reptile?

A reptile is a scaly skinned creature, such as a lizard, snake, turtle, tortoise, alligator, or crocodile. The easiest way to tell the difference between a reptile and an amphibian is to touch them. The skin of reptiles is dry rather than moist, and tough. This protects them from attack and guards against water loss.

Like amphibians, reptiles also lay eggs, but on land, so their young are not raised in the water. An egg with a fluid-filled sac (called an amniotic sac) around the embryo provides nourishment for the baby reptile, while the egg's hard shell protects it from attack. A miniature adult

Fascinating Fact

Some rain forest snakes have evolved on separate continents, thousands of miles apart, yet they are almost identical.

THE PYGMY MARSUPIAL FROG

Most frogs and toads lay their eggs in water, where they remain until they hatch. Some frogs and toads, however, have developed unusual ways of caring for their eggs.

The pygmy marsupial frog comes from Venezuela. After the male has mated with the female, she produces eggs. The male then places the eggs in a special sac on the female's back where they are kept moist, rather like being in water. The eggs develop into tadpoles in the sac. When they are a few weeks old, the female releases her tadpoles (see left) into a pool of water to complete their development from tadpoles into frogs.

emerges from the egg and can begin a life similar to an adult's right away. Reptiles are less dependent on water than are amphibians, but spend their lives partly in water and partly on dry land.

As a young reptile grows bigger, it sheds its skin to reveal a new skin underneath. Reptiles continue to grow and shed their skins throughout their lives.

▶ The dry, scaly skin of this anaconda snake from the Amazon rain forest is typical of the skin of a reptile.

Keeping a Regular Temperature

A warm-blooded creature, such as a mammal or a bird, is able to maintain a fairly constant body temperature whether its environment is hot or cold. It eats frequently to provide the energy necessary to maintain this regular level. Because reptiles and amphibians are cold-blooded, however, they cannot keep their body at an even temperature. Instead, they are affected by the temperature of their surroundings. Reptiles and amphibians have to try to maintain a consistent temperature level by moving in and out of sunlight, shade, or water. They must avoid getting too hot or too cold so that their body organs can function well.

▲ In order to warm itself up, an Amazonian lizard basks in a patch of sunlight on the forest floor.

▼ Cold-blooded reptiles such as caimans eat far less often than warm-blooded mammals or birds.

THE AMAZONIAN RIVER TURTLE

After a cool night, the Amazonian river turtle will climb onto a log to warm up. It extends its neck and feet as far as possible to catch as much warmth as it can. Gradually, the turtle's body temperature begins to rise until all the internal organs are functioning well. The turtle may then plunge into the water to look for food. After a while in the cool water, its body temperature begins to drop. The turtle then finds another log to bask on, repeating the process of warming up and cooling down several times a day.

The advantage of not having to use energy to maintain their body temperature is that reptiles can live on very little food. A snake, for example, needs only one-tenth to one-hundredth of the food required for a mammal or bird of the same weight.

Keeping Warm and Cooling Down

Rain forests are ideal environments for amphibians and reptiles because they maintain fairly constant temperatures. After a cool night, however, reptiles and amphibians need to get warm. They usually do this by lying in the sun.

Many reptiles and amphibians turn a darker color in order to absorb the sun's warmth better. Once they are warm enough, their bodies become more active and they may look for food. When they need to cool down, some species of reptile and amphibian become paler to reflect the heat. They may take a dip in the water, or crawl into the shade of the rain forest, emerging only in the cool of the evening. At night, reptiles and amphibians usually sleep, but some small species of lizard (called geckos), like the New Caledonian crested gecko, and snake, such as the West African night adder, are active on warm nights.

② DIVERSITY

The Range of Amphibians and Reptiles

Amphibians appeared on Earth around 370 million years ago and were descended from a group of lobe-finned bony fish. Reptiles evolved from amphibians around 315 million years ago and went on to develop into hundreds of different types of animal. These included the dinosaurs that dominated life on Earth for millions of years. Of the twenty different groups or orders of reptile that existed in prehistoric times, only five exist today. Four of these orders are found in the rain forests.

Groups of Amphibians and Reptiles

There are believed to be around 4,200 species of amphibian and 6,400 species of reptile living in the world today.

▼ Many reptiles, such as this sail-finned lizard, resemble the dinosaur.

RAIN FOREST SECRETS

THE AGE OF THE DINOSAURS

This is the fossil of an allosaurus, which was a fierce carnivorous reptile 34 feet (10.4 m) in length. It existed when the dinosaurs dominated the planet about 220 million years ago. So far, fossils of more than 500 different species have been unearthed, but there were probably hundreds more species that have not yet been discovered.

The "age of the dinosaurs" lasted for more than 160 million years, before they became extinct. No one is exactly sure why the dinosaurs died out or why the types of reptile that exist today survived. Dinosaurs may have become extinct because of a drop in temperature. Small aquatic reptiles could have survived because the temperature of fresh water in lakes and streams does not vary as greatly as temperatures on land. In addition, small reptiles on land could warm up more quickly than the giant dinosaurs.

The chameleon is a slow-moving lizard that lives in trees. Chameleons are found mainly in Africa and Madagascar.

This yellow caiman is part of the order of crocodilians, which includes alligators and crocodiles.

The rain forests are believed to contain around two-thirds of all these species of reptile and amphibian. Rain forest varieties range from saltwater crocodiles weighing more than 2,100 pounds (950 kg) to miniature Amazonian lizards weighing just a fraction of an ounce.

Reptiles and amphibians can each be divided into different groups. Amphibians can be divided into three main groups, or orders. Two of these groups—salamanders and newts, and frogs and toads—are all four-legged. But the third group of amphibian, which is called caecilians, have no legs at all. Their tubular, jointed bodies make them look rather like worms. Rain forest reptiles fall into four main groups—lizards, snakes, turtles and tortoises, and crocodilians. The crocodilian group includes alligators, crocodiles, and caimans.

▼ *A typical frog that lives on the forest floor. It has smooth moist skin and long legs for jumping. Its brown color helps it hide easily among dead leaves.*

Frogs and Toads

There are about 4,000 species of frog and toad worldwide. The main difference between frogs and toads is their appearance. Frogs often have smooth, moist skin and long legs, while toads have drier, warty skin and shorter legs.

Many species of frog and toad are found in the rain forests. Amazonian tree frogs, which weigh only a fraction of an ounce, are tiny compared with giant toads such as the goliath toad from Africa. This huge toad can measure over 12 inches (300 mm) in length and weigh up to 8 pounds (3.5 kg).

RAIN FOREST SECRETS

THE GIANT TOAD

The giant toad, sometimes called the cane toad, is one of the largest toads in the world. It can measure over 9 inches (240 mm) in length. It lives in many types of tropical habitat and feeds on a wide variety of food, including insects (particularly beetles) and mammals such as small rodents, opossums, and small birds.

The giant toad protects itself by secreting poisonous chemicals through its skin, which are deadly to many mammal predators.

Giant toads can breed at any time of the year. The female lays up to 350,000 eggs in the water each year, many of which are eaten by predators.

▲ Like many other species, this salamander from Costa Rica in Central America is brightly colored to let predators know that it is poisonous.

▼ Caecilians, like this one from West Africa, are often confused with snakes or worms because of their cylindrical, legless bodies and their burrowing lifestyle.

Salamanders and Newts

There are about 360 species of salamander and newt. However, it is likely that there are many more species living in the rain forests that we have not yet discovered. Most salamanders and newts are brightly colored and about 4 to 6 inches (100–150 mm) long, but some of the largest species can be over 3 feet (1 m) in length. Some species of salamander have no lungs, such as the tlaconete salamander that lives in the tropical montane forests of Central Mexico. It breathes through its moist skin.

Caecilians

There are about 160–170 species of caecilians and they all live in tropical climates. These unusual amphibians spend most of their lives underground. Their bodies are ideally suited for burrowing under the soil. They have thick skulls, and their eyes and mouths are sunken to avoid taking in too much earth as they burrow for worms and insects.

15

▼ *The green iguana of South and Central America is one of the most familiar types of rain forest lizard. It is well suited to climbing among the trees.*

Lizards

There are an estimated 4,000 species of lizard worldwide—more than all the other types of reptiles combined. Many live in the rain forests. Lizards have long bodies covered with overlapping scales and most species have legs. Some lizards, such as chameleons, move very slowly and use their tail like a limb to help them grip tree branches. Others, such as basilisk lizards, run fast on their two hind legs. The flying dragon can extend its wing-like flaps so it glides between trees, while the Madagascan day gecko has developed sticky pads on its toes to help it cling to flat surfaces.

RAIN FOREST SECRETS

TOKAY GECKO LIZARD

The tokay gecko is a brightly colored lizard from Southeast Asia. Like all geckos, it has many miniature suction pads on its toes to help it walk along smooth, flat surfaces. It catches insects, such as flies and cockroaches, using its long, sticky tongue.

The habitat of the tokay gecko has been greatly reduced as rain forests have been turned into agricultural land and towns and cities have expanded. However, the tokay gecko has adapted to living in houses. Its special toes mean that it can hunt upside down on the ceiling of homes. Because the tokay gecko hunts insect pests, most people tolerate its living in their environment.

▶ *South American boa constrictors like this one can kill prey as large as a pig by using special techniques.*

Fascinating Fact

Snakes hunt by sight, sound, and smell. They have no ears but they pick up vibrations from the ground and can smell with their tongue.

Snakes

Snakes are reptiles that do not have limbs. There are around 2,500 species of snake, but the largest, and some of the most colorful, are found in rain forests. The boa constrictor from the Amazon rain forest, for example, can reach lengths of 30 feet (9 m), while an adult brahimy blind snake from Southeast Asia grows to only four inches (110 mm) long. The range of colors and patterns varies, from the well camouflaged tree snake such as the red-tailed racer, to the brightly colored red-, black-, and yellow-banded coral snake.

Snakes have different ways of catching and killing their prey, but they usually swallow it whole. Snakes have evolved elasticated tendons on their jaws, which allows them to open their mouths very wide to swallow food that is much larger than the snakes themselves.

▼ *Turtles, such as this species of Amazonian river turtle, are excellent swimmers and spend most of their lives in or near the water.*

▼ *Tortoises, such as this species of African tortoise, spend their entire lives on dry land and forage among the leaf litter on the forest floor.*

Turtles and Tortoises

Turtles and tortoises have existed in roughly the same form for more than 200 million years. Today, there are around 250 species of turtle and tortoise, mainly living in rivers in the tropical rain forests. Turtles and tortoises have soft bodies that are protected inside a hard bony shell. They do not have teeth but bite with a horny beak that covers their mouth.

Turtles and tortoises have adapted to their rain forest environments in different ways.

RAIN FOREST SECRETS

THE MATAMATA TURTLE

Matamata turtles are found in dark-water rivers and stagnant pools in the South American countries of Brazil, Colombia, and Venezuela. The matamata turtle is one of the most curious-looking of all turtles. It is one of a number of species of turtle that have long, slender noses, which they use like snorkels to remain hidden underwater. The matamata is well camouflaged with a rough, ridged shell that looks like a piece of tree bark. It has a flattened head with loose flaps of skin that resemble the color and shape of fallen leaves.

Matamata turtles feed on small fish that are fooled by their camouflage. When the fish swim close to the turtle's mouth, they are gulped down.

Turtles are often aquatic while tortoises usually live on land. There is a huge variety in both size and pattern. Leatherback turtles can reach sizes of over 6 feet (2 m) in length, while Amazonian axe turtles can be as small as 5.5 inches long (140 mm) when they are fully grown.

Crocodilians

Crocodilians are a group of 22 reptile species. These are very large reptiles that have bony plates, like armor, along their backs. Crocodilians usually have long tails and short legs. Their mouths are made up of huge, powerful jaws, lined with sharp teeth.

The crocodilian group includes the largest reptiles alive today. Some can grow to 23 feet (7 m) in length and weigh nearly 2,200 pounds (1,000 kg). Crocodilians are powerful swimmers but tend to be clumsy on land. Since they spend most of their time in the water, crocodilians have eyes and nostrils set

▲ The spectacled caiman has powerful jaws and eyes set high on its head. This means it can float almost completely hidden underwater and still watch for unsuspecting prey.

high on their heads to remain above the water while the rest of the animal is submerged. They are all carnivorous predators and lie in wait for their prey.

The main differences between crocodiles and alligators (including caimans) are the width of their snouts and their number of teeth. Alligators have wider, more rounded snouts than crocodiles, whose are thinner and squarer. Crocodiles have an extra tooth on each side of the lower jaw, visible when the jaw is closed.

Types of Rain Forest

Rain forests found in different parts of the world often look quite similar to each other. However, each is unique and contains different combinations of reptiles and amphibians.

Scientists recognize more than forty different types of rain forest. The most widespread type is the lowland forest, which includes the Amazon rain forest in Brazil. Here, the main division is between *terra firme* (dry ground forest) and *várzea* (flooded forest), which is underwater for several months of each year. Another important type of lowland rain forest is the mangrove forest, which lies along tropical coastlines. The higher tropical montane forests are cooler and wetter than the lowland forests.

▲ A small Amazonian iguana clings to the roots of a rain forest fig tree in the flooded forest (várzea) of the Amazon in Brazil.

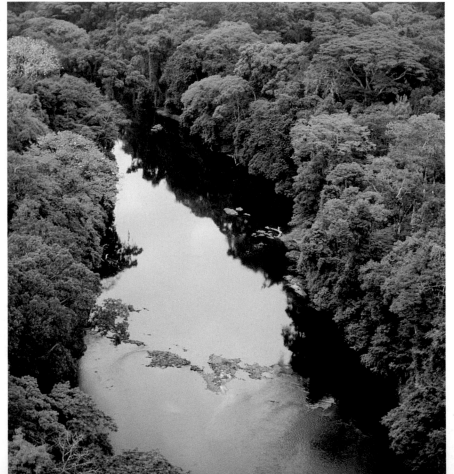

◀ Rivers, lakes, and even pools in the hollows of trees provide an ideal habitat for thousands of species of rain forest reptile and amphibian.

Layers of the Rain Forest

There are varied habitats in each of the different layers of rain forest, from the canopy down to the forest floor. Some species of lizard, such as the Amazonian iguana, can move from the rain forest floor to the understory and intermediate layers—and even bask in the tropical sunshine in the emergent trees above the canopy.

Others, such as the many species of tree frog, can live out their entire lives in a single bromeliad plant high in the canopy. Tree snakes slither through the middle layers of rain forest where they locate prey with their heat sensors. Tortoises live on the forest floor, while the moist tropical soils provide a home for caecilians. Rivers and lakes are excellent habitats for species of turtle, crocodilian, and aquatic snake.

▼ *Snakes and iguanas can often be seen on the tallest trees basking in the sun to get warm.*

POOLS IN THE SKY

Tree frogs live high up in the canopy of rain forest trees. When they want to breed, some frogs slowly make their way down the tree trunks to rain forest pools. Their long legs and sticky toe pads help them to climb downward.

Smaller tree frogs may spend their entire lives in the canopy. When these tree frogs breed, their tadpoles need to spend the early part of their lives in water. In many rain forests of South and Central America, bromeliads grow on the branches and trunks of trees high in the canopy. The leaves of the bromeliads form a rosette in the center of the plant and collect water. It is in these "pools in the sky" that frogs such as the strawberry poison-arrow frog release their tadpoles, which they have carried on their backs since hatching. The strawberry poison-arrow frog is unusual because it feeds its young with eggs that never hatched.

Mangrove Forest

Mangrove forest grows in the mud at the edges of seas and rivers. It is home to many reptiles and amphibians, such as the saltwater crocodile of northern Australia and the mangrove pit viper of Asia. There are a number of different types of mangrove forest around the world, covering an area of about 930 square miles (2,400 sq km). Sea snakes, lizards, and green turtles hunt for small insects, crustaceans, and small fish among the bell-shaped roots of mangrove trees.

▲ Mangrove forest, such as this one in Tanzania, lines about a quarter of the world's tropical coastlines.

► Mangroves are home to some very rare reptiles and amphibians such as this mangrove pit viper.

MADAGASCAN TREE BOA

Despite its name, the Madagascan tree boa spends as much time on the forest floor as it does in the trees of the tropical montane forests of eastern Madagascar. Because tropical montane forest is cooler than lowland forest, this tree snake is often seen on the forest floor where it is either basking in the sun to warm up or digesting its last meal. The tree boa is the smallest and most commonly found boa in Madagascar. Tree boas are usually olive green and black with a shiny blue gloss, except for the young snakes, which are bright orange and red.

The Madagascan tree boa feeds mainly on warm-blooded prey.

The snake kills its prey by winding its body around it to strangle it, then swallowing it whole. The boa has a row of heat-sensitive sensors around its lips to help locate its warm-blooded prey in the dark.

▼ A chameleon sits and waits for prey in a tree in Madagascar's tropical montane forest.

Tropical Montane Forest

There are many species of reptile and amphibian that have adapted to life in the cooler conditions of the tropical montane forests. These forests are found in South American countries such as Venezuela and Colombia, Irian Jaya in Asia, and Rwanda in Africa. Tropical montane forest trees are covered in many types of epiphytes—plants that grow on the trunks and branches. These plants, including orchids and bromeliads, are home to many types of insect, providing a source of food for frogs, lizards, and tree snakes. Some species of reptile and amphibian can be found as high as 13,000 feet (4,000 m), where trees are stunted and temperatures are only slightly above freezing.

Predators

All adult amphibians and most reptiles are predators—they catch and eat other animals. If necessary, reptiles and amphibians can survive for long periods of time without food. A large crocodile or snake can sometimes go for several weeks or even months between meals. While some reptiles and amphibians eat almost anything they can catch, most species have very specific diets.

Carnivorous Amphibians

All adult amphibians are carnivorous. Their diet includes insects, reptiles, small mammals, and fish, but they have only a few ways of catching their prey. The most common method for frogs, toads, salamanders, and newts is to use their long, prehensile tongue with a sticky end.

▲ *The skink is a reptile that feeds mainly on insects. All skinks have short limbs, and some may have a prehensile tail.*

▼ *This small lizard lives in the Amazon rain forest and preys mainly on insects.*

MADAGASCAN CHAMELEONS

A chameleon is an expert insect hunter. It moves slowly through the rain forest with a rocking motion, waiting for an unsuspecting insect to draw near. When an insect is close, the chameleon flicks out its sticky tongue at lightning speed and captures the insect by dragging it into its mouth.

Over half of all the 135 species of chameleon that are known to exist are found in Madagascar. They are perfectly adapted to living in trees and usually have thin bodies to help them move between the tangle of branches, twigs, and thorns. Their clamp-like feet give them a good hold on small branches. Most chameleons are greenish, but many can change their color and patterning to hide among the leaves.

Chameleons have the unusual ability to move their eyes independently of each other, which allows them to look around while remaining motionless in a tree.

However, both eyes focus together when the chameleon spots its prey so that it can accurately land its sticky tongue on the insect, which it eats in an instant.

This is aimed at the prey with explosive speed. The victim enters the open mouth as the tongue recoils. The other way of catching food is by gulping it into a large mouth. Large amphibians such as the African bullfrog use this method to catch small mammals. Aquatic amphibians also catch prey that live in water by this technique. Like all amphibians, caecilians are toothless, and swallow their prey whole.

Carnivorous Reptiles

Most reptiles are carnivorous. They have evolved a number of different methods for catching prey. A few lizards use their long, sticky tongue in the same way as amphibians, but most do not. Some snakes can catch a victim with either their fangs or their sharp teeth.

◄ *The rows of teeth of this yellow caiman indicate that it is a carnivorous predator.*

RAIN FOREST SECRETS

THE EYELASH VIPER

One of the most beautiful and deadly predators of South and Central America is the eyelash viper. Eyelash vipers are typically small, growing to lengths of between 16–24 inches (400–600 mm). They belong to the most advanced group of venomous snake— the pit viper. This means that they have special folding, tubular fangs set at the front of the mouth to inject their deadly venom.

Pit vipers are usually nocturnal and feed on frogs, lizards, birds, and small mammals. They have a wide range of colors and patterning, from a uniform brown to brilliant yellow, red, green, or gray with contrasting spots. They are superb predators and are well camouflaged on the flowers and fruits of a number of rain forest plants. They are so quick that they can strike even at fast-moving prey. This eyelash viper (see right) is lying in wait for a hummingbird to arrive and feed at the heliconia plant.

Others immobilize a victim with a venomous bite. Some snakes crush the air out of their prey until it has suffocated. Crocodiles and alligators usually drown their victims. They often let their prey partly decompose underwater before tearing it into bite-size pieces by seizing it in their jaws and spinning rapidly in the water.

▲ There are two different species of Amazonian river turtle sitting on this log. They both eat mainly plant material and only occasionally feed on insects and small fish.

Herbivores and Omnivores

There are only a few reptiles and a small number of species of lizard, turtle, and tortoise that are herbivores. The largest of these is the green iguana, which can grow to 6 feet (almost 2 m) in length, and has a diet of mainly leaves and fruit. Other species of lizard, such as the rhinoceros iguana, live on seaweed alone. There are also types of land-living tortoises that are herbivores. Most reptiles are omnivores, however, and eat insects, slugs, and fish in addition to plant material. This includes many species of lizard, turtle, and tortoise. Different species of the South American river turtle eat mainly plants but may occasionally supplement their diet with other foods.

Camouflage

Many species of amphibian and reptile can blend into the rain forest background. Amazonian frogs, which hop along the forest floor, are similar in color and shape to fallen leaves. The colors of the fringed geckos of Madagascar resemble the patterning of the bark of the trees they usually live on. Even large lizards such as the green iguana, which is about a yard (meter) long, are difficult to see because their green bodies match the surrounding foliage. Many tree snakes are green so they can hide themselves away in the rain forest. Most frogs and toads also have the ability to change their color to help them remain camouflaged. Tree frogs, including White's tree frog, can be dark brown or green when on the bark of a tree and pale leaf-green when among the foliage.

▲ An Amazonian lizard blends in almost perfectly with its background because of its speckled camouflage colors.

◄ Some rain forest frogs are not only the same color as the background leaves they hide among, but their shape is the same as the leaves.

Poisons

Many types of frog and salamander are brilliantly colored to advertise the fact that they are poisonous. This warns a predator that it could die a painful death if it tried to eat

Fascinating Fact

A minute amount of poison from a poison-arrow frog could kill a mammal as large as a jaguar.

one of these amphibians. Poison-arrow frogs secrete poisons through their skin while the giant toad has poison glands on its back, which it uses to squirt poison at its attacker. Some salamanders have poison glands on their heads and they swing their heads around wildly, trying to butt and poison their attacker. Some newts have poison glands in their tails and whip their attacker with it to defend themselves.

Some snakes and lizards produce foul-tasting liquids as a deterrent against predators that may try to eat them.

▲ The brightly colored coral snake is one of the most poisonous snakes in the world.

RAIN FOREST SECRETS

THE POISON-ARROW FROG

This poison-arrow frog from the Amazon has beautiful, colorful markings. The colors tell predators that these small frogs are deadly poisonous. The Kokoi poison-arrow frog of Colombia, for example, can produce a poison that can be absorbed through the skin of a predator. A minute amount is enough to kill a human being. Indigenous people in South and Central America use the poisonous secretions from local species of poison-arrow frog to tip their blow-pipe darts and arrows when hunting. It is from this hunting activity that the poison-arrow frog got its name.

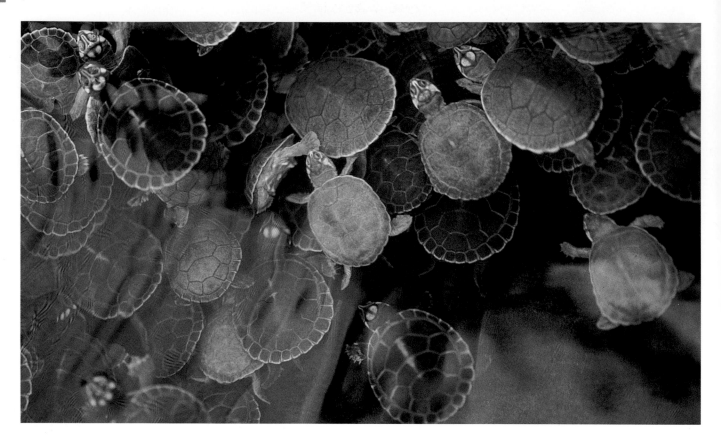

Protective Bodies

Many reptiles have developed special shells or scales to help protect them from attack. Tortoises and turtles, for example, have a hard shell. When threatened, they can withdraw their head and legs into their shells and out of danger. Many crocodilians have armored, bony scales along their backs to protect them from attack, often from larger individuals of the same species. Large lizards, such as sail-finned lizards or iguanas, often display a ridge of bony, and sometimes sharp, scales along their backs.

The skin of all reptiles is impermeable, which means they do not lose water through their skin as amphibians do. The tough, scaly skins of snakes not only help keep in water but also protect the snake from attack. However, these skins are shed to permit the snake to grow. When a snake is young, it will shed its skin more often as it grows rapidly.

▲ *Like land-living tortoises, these turtles run the greatest risk of attack by predators during the first few weeks of their lives when their shells are still soft.*

Fascinating Fact

Some species of lizard have a tail that breaks off when it is grabbed by a predator. These lizards also have the ability to grow a new one.

THE BASILISK

This striking lizard usually lives in the tangled plants at the edges of streams in parts of Central America. It eats insects, snails, and small fish, and relies on camouflage both for hunting and for avoiding predators.

When threatened, the basilisk has a very special means of escape. It rears up on its back legs and runs away at remarkable speed. It can run very fast on the ground, but it can also run away over water on its webbed hind feet.

It is thought that the lizard is kept afloat by its speed, while its long tail helps maintain balance.

Making a Swift Escape

Reptiles and amphibians are experts at jumping away from danger. Frogs regularly avoid attack by making large leaps powered by their muscular back legs. Flying frogs glide through the air, stopping their fall with their webbed feet and hanging on to branches with their sticky pads. Crocodiles, alligators, and snakes can all move fast over short distances. Lizards can make fast getaways, sprinting out of danger on their back legs.

◄ This rhinoceros iguana is about a yard long. If it is threatened by a predator, it can move very quickly on its strong legs, despite its large size.

31

5 DISAPPEARING SPECIES

Why Are Reptiles and Amphibians Disappearing?
The number of many species of rain forest reptile and amphibian has declined rapidly over the last twenty years. The golden toad from Costa Rica, for example, is thought to be extinct. Tree frogs, spectacled cobras, black caimans, and leatherback turtles have all declined and are now under threat.

The largest single cause for the decline of reptiles and amphibians is the destruction of their habitat. They are also sensitive to changes in environmental conditions caused by pollution. They are vulnerable to changes in the local climate caused by global warming, which is the result of human activity through industrial processes.

▲ A golden toad from Costa Rica. Golden toads were once considered common. Twenty years later they are now believed to be extinct because of changes in their environment.

Fascinating Fact

Scientists believe that chemicals that cause pollution are stopping many rare species from being able to breed properly.

◄ In the Amazon rain forest, tortoises are often trapped by local people for food.

▲ *The capture of many reptiles for pets, including iguanas, has drastically reduced their numbers in the wild.*

The Pet Trade

Many species of reptile are also caught for the pet trade. Rare species of animal can be worth tens of thousands of dollars in trade around the world. Every year, many thousands of rain forest amphibians and reptiles are caught for the international pet trade. Chinese water dragons (a type of lizard), boa constrictors, rare tree frogs, and many other rain forest reptiles and amphibians are being sold in ever increasing numbers. Large reptiles, such as iguanas and Amazonian caimans, are being offered today as pets in many of the world's richer countries.

LINKS

White's Tree Frog

White's tree frog comes from the rain forests of Australia. This dumpy tree frog has become a popular pet. It changes color as it moves from leaves to tree trunks or onto the ground, which makes it very appealing. It is also popular because it is friendly, and can become tame. Some frogs can be trained to feed from the hand of their owner.

However, the popularity of the frog as a pet in the homes of people in North America and Europe has led to a massive decline in the number of frogs in the wild. White's tree frogs are protected by international law and are officially protected in the rain forests of Australia. Frogs bred in captivity are now supplying the demand of pet stores, helping to keep up the numbers of this species in the rain forests.

Hunting for Food

Many indigenous peoples in the tropical rain forests have hunted reptiles and amphibians for food for thousands of years. The smoky mountain frog is known as "the chicken of the forest" and is a regular part of the diet of some rain forest people in Central America. Reptiles such as green iguanas also form an important part of people's diet. Over the last century, millions of settlers have moved into rain forests and now some reptile species, such as the green iguana, are threatened. Some species of Amazonian river turtle, which once lined the main rivers in the millions, have now been hunted almost to extinction in large parts of the rain forest. In parts of the world such as the Far East, snake meat and turtle eggs are popular foods.

▲ The smoky mountain frog is commonly eaten by people who live in Central American countries such as Panama.

◄ Children helping to roast the turtles that their father caught during the night in an Amazon settlement near Manaus, Brazil.

LINKS

Iguana Project

After years of being hunted and with the demand for its meat increasing, the green iguana is in danger of becoming extinct in many areas. Special projects in Panama, Costa Rica, and Mexico have been started where farmers have been encouraged to breed and "farm" iguanas for food. Many small-scale farmers have taken up the idea and now breed iguanas (see right). Iguanas can produce as much meat per acre as cattle, but at a fraction of the cost. This helps local people provide for themselves without over-hunting wild iguanas in the rain forest.

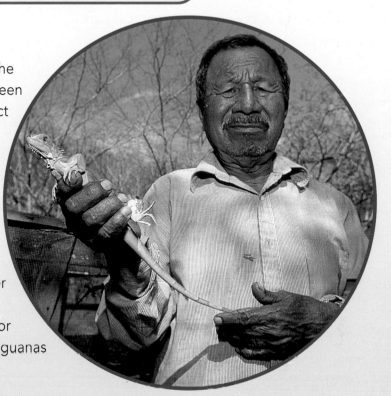

Skin Trade

The hunting of animals for their skins has caused reptile numbers to decline in the rain forests. Spectacled cobras from Thailand, boa constrictors and caimans from South America, and many other types of reptiles have very valuable skins, and have been hunted heavily. The rarer the skin of the reptile, the more people will be prepared to pay for it. Killing endangered reptiles continues, even though it is often illegal to do so. For poor people in the rain forest, selling skins is one way to earn money to feed their families. On a bigger scale, criminal organizations often smuggle skins to wealthy buyers in the developed countries of the world.

◀ *Caiman skins are valuable and caimans are often hunted to increase a family's income.*

Disappearing Habitats

Tropical rain forests have a greater variety of species of amphibian and reptile than any other type of habitat. When they are destroyed, many species become extinct. Huge areas of rain forest are being cut down for timber, firewood, charcoal, and wood pulp for paper. Vast areas are also being converted into agricultural land. Soybean production in the Amazon rain forest, African oil palm plantations in West Africa, and rice cultivation in Asia have caused the loss of millions of acres of rain forest. The building of dams and mines and the expansion of towns and cities have also led to rain forest loss. Not only are huge areas of rain forest being burned and destroyed, but they are also becoming fragmented. This makes it more difficult for animals such as turtles to migrate to their breeding grounds.

Pollution

Today, there are higher levels of pollution than ever before. Toxic gases are produced by factories, and human and chemical waste is found in almost all the world's seas, rivers, and lakes.

Amphibians are easily harmed by pollutants because their thin skins readily absorb chemicals

◀ Large commercial operations such as mining have destroyed and polluted large areas of rain forest. This means that many local species of reptile and amphibian no longer exist.

▼ The skin of all frogs is thin and is designed to absorb water and oxygen from the atmosphere. Frogs can die if pollution from the atmosphere is absorbed through their skin.

Dangers to Leatherback Turtles

The leatherback turtle (see right) is the largest of all turtles, growing to over 6 feet long (2 m) and weighing more than 1,850 pounds (850 kg) when fully grown. Many turtles nest on beaches near mangrove forests and hunt in the shallow coastal waters of rain forest islands. Different species of leatherback turtle can easily swim the width of the Atlantic or Pacific oceans, which they do on their annual migrations.

Ocean-going turtles experience different dangers from those that live only in rain forest rivers and streams. Leatherbacks often get caught up and drown in the huge nets used to catch commercial fish, such as tuna, at sea. They are also known to have died because they mistake plastic bags for jellyfish. Excellent beaches often attract the development of holiday resorts, which displace the nesting turtles.

▼ *Waterborne chemicals can easily pass through the skins of tadpoles, preventing them from developing properly.*

from their surroundings. For example, mercury has been released into Amazonian rivers by gold miners in recent years. This can prevent tadpoles from developing normally as they grow. Pollutants can also poison fish, which, in turn, poison the reptiles that eat fish from the rivers. Similarly, reptiles and amphibians eat insects, which may have been in contact with DDT, a pesticide used to keep down the numbers of insects in the tropics. Nobody knows the long-term effects of DDT on reptiles and amphibians.

◀ *The habitats of many rare species of reptile and amphibian are being lost as logging companies cut down the rain forests.*

Saving the Species

No one knows exactly by how much the wild populations of rain forest amphibians and reptiles have declined or how many species have become extinct. All that is certain is that without conservation projects, the number of extinctions per year will continue to rise. Fortunately, there are many concerned individuals and environmental organizations that are fighting hard for a better future for reptiles and amphibians. By far, the most serious problem is destruction of the rain forest. Many development and environmental organizations are campaigning to reduce the rate at which the world's rain forests are lost. Many rain forest communities are receiving education on how to find alternative employment for people now working in the destructive industries of logging, cattle farming, and hunting. Other problems are being tackled, such as hunting for

▼ *In many countries such as Brazil, there are park guards who help look after the rain forest.*

Preventing Illegal Imports

At major international airports such as Heathrow in London, there are specially trained customs officers that try to prevent the importing of endangered reptiles and other species. Every week, customs officers may find anything from live turtles and snakes to items such as caiman-skin handbags (see right).

Customs officers act according to international laws set under an agreement aimed at reducing the trade of rare and endangered species. One of the top three destinations in the world for both legal and illegal imports is Great Britain. World Wildlife Fund campaigns to highlight the problem of illegally imported goods.

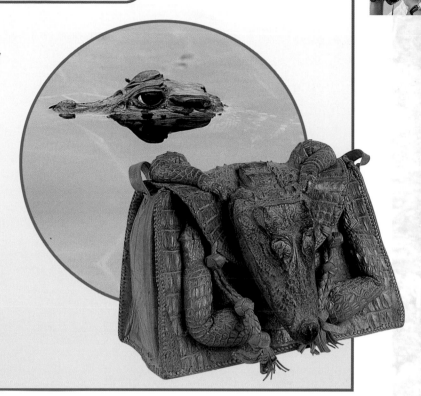

skins and collecting animals for medicines. Environmental organizations are promoting international laws to protect rare species, and trying to reduce pollution.

Fascinating Fact

It is estimated that 100 million reptile skins are traded legally and illegally each year.

Protected Areas

One of the ways of helping rare rain forest reptiles and amphibians to survive is to protect the rain forests in which they live. If the areas are large enough, many species of rare amphibian and reptile have a good chance of survival. Organizations such as WWF (World Wildlife Fund) have successfully campaigned for protected areas to be set up all over the world. These can take the form of national parks, nature reserves, community managed land, rain forest reserves, certified rain forest areas, and rain forest corridors that link large areas of rain forest. There are very few areas specifically protected for amphibians and reptiles. However, if areas are set up to protect rare birds or mammals, this means that reptiles and amphibians can benefit as well.

Research

Conservation projects can only be effective if they are based on good research. The lives of many rain forest amphibians and reptiles are complicated. It can take researchers years to begin to understand an animal's role in an ecosystem and what needs to be done to protect it from becoming extinct.

Scientists carry out research to estimate the numbers of rare animals, and to study how particular animals respond to changes in their habitats. For example, some rare species such as the egg-eating snake rely on one specific type of food. Others require special habitats in order to reproduce, such as the tree frogs that lay their eggs in the water contained in bromeliad plants. By studying what some rare species need to survive, scientists can advise conservation organizations about the type of rain forest that needs to be protected and the actions they should take.

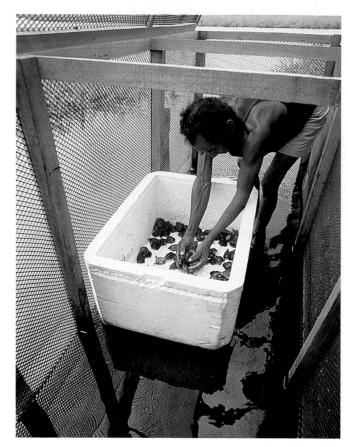

▲ The breeding of turtles in captivity is one way of helping to restore numbers to an area of rain forest.

▼ Mucus from the back of the Brazilian bicolored tree frog may be useful in medical research.

Reptiles for Medicine

Rain forest reptiles and amphibians are important in the research and development of medicines. The poisonous and foul-smelling secretions produced by frogs and toads have been shown to have many medical applications, from painkillers to antibiotics.

Mamiraua—A Model for Conservation

The setting up of the Mamiraua ecological reserve in the state of Amazonas in Brazil in 1992 has provided a model for conservation in the Amazon. The reserve covers 2,777,500 acres (1,124,000 hectares) of flooded forest, creating a protected area where local people and wildlife live side by side.

In the reserve, the people live a traditional lifestyle, collecting rain forest fruits and seeds, fishing, and hunting animals such as turtles. However, the level of these activities is closely controlled so they do not damage the rain forest ecosystem. Mamiraua also has legal protection against poaching. The numbers of rare black caimans and Amazonian river turtles (see right) have been increasing ever since the establishment of the reserve.

The Brazilian bicolored tree frog, for example, produces a special mucus that affects how well nerve cells function. This may help in treating diseases related to the brain or nervous system in humans. The venoms from many deadly snakes have also been shown to reduce high blood pressure and improve the consistency of a person's blood.

The chemicals that help some amphibians and reptiles to grow a limb or tail after being attacked are also being studied for possible use in transplant surgery. Some snakes are captured and samples of their venom taken, before they are released again. Chemists need only small amounts to work out the chemical structure of the active ingredient, which they can later manufacture themselves.

Education

Education is an important part of conservation. Large landowners often destroy the rain forest they own or drain important wetland and mangrove habitats for agriculture and ranching. With better education, they could cause far less damage and give themselves a better income. They could work in ecotourism, or collect sustainable products such as palm fruits and nuts. Many small rain forest communities can learn about how to conserve rain forest resources in ways that do not harm the environment, but preserve it for the future.

▲ A sign for the national park in Madagascar, which was set up for the protection of all wildlife that lives within it.

LINKS

Children of the Flooded Forest

These are children from the villages of San Juan and Aracampinas in the flooded forest near the Amazonian town of Santarem. They are learning about the local environment in their lessons at school. One of their practical projects arose from talking to the older members of their villages about what life was like fifty years ago. They discovered that there are very few turtles seen in the rivers today compared with only a few decades ago.

In 2000, the children decided to organize their own captive breeding project. Turtle eggs were collected from the local beaches, and the turtles were raised until they were mature enough to look after themselves (see below). This project should lead to an increase in the number of turtles locally.

Organizations such as WWF and Friends of the Earth support many environmental education projects in schools, in the hope that the next generation will be better informed about how to look after the natural world around it. Students can learn about different species that live in the rain forests, such as snakes, so they can avoid the unnecessary killing of harmless reptiles. Environmental education is also important for children in non-rain forest countries so that they become aware of what they can be done to help save rare amphibians and reptiles from extinction.

▼ *The protection of the habitat of the estuarine crocodile in Australia has led to a huge increase in numbers.*

International Law

Over the last few decades, wildlife has been given much more protection by the introduction of new international and national laws. In many countries, there are laws that aim to stop the hunting of rare mammals. There are also special international laws to prevent all rare animal products and skins—including the skins of snakes and frogs—from being traded around the world. The International Convention for the Trade in Endangered Species

(CITES) is an agreement that encourages countries to help protect rare species from becoming extinct. CITES maintains a list of endangered amphibian and reptile species that are illegal to traffic. The law has been very successful for some rare species. The population of reptiles, such as the estuarine crocodile in Queensland, Australia, has recovered so well that there are almost too many. The creeks close to the ocean have now become dangerous for tourists.

7 THE FUTURE

The Problems

The future for rain forest reptiles and amphibians looks uncertain. The rain forests in which they live are being destroyed faster than ever before, and other human activities are also pushing many reptile and amphibian species to the brink of extinction. Pollution of the rivers and lakes is causing a drastic decline in wild populations, and the introduction of alien species has also devastated local reptile and amphibian populations. Many reptiles and amphibians live in very specific conditions and if these trends continue, the only future for many species may well be in zoos and scientific institutions.

▲ It is important that rare crocodilians are protected to ensure their survival in the future.

▼ Captive breeding and release into the wild may help increase the numbers of endangered reptiles and amphibians.

A Positive Response

Fortunately, more and more people are taking an interest in protecting as many different species as possible. Environmental organizations such as WWF have been campaigning for the world's governments to

Ecotourism

Madagascar has thousands of unique species of reptiles and amphibians in its rain forests. Today, tourists are eager to pay to visit a rain forest to see unusual creatures. About 150 miles from the capital of Madagascar is a national park. People come to visit the park from all over the world. They are not only interested in its population of lemurs, but also Madagascar's unique species of amphibians and reptiles. Chameleon tours are particularly popular with the tourists.

Around 95 percent of Madagascar's rain forest has been destroyed. People have lost not only this habitat but also the opportunity to make a living from it.

The national park, however, employs many local people, and the local community is benefiting from the money that comes from this tourist industry.

▼ This Amazonian tree frog sits camouflaged on a branch. It is a local species, not widely known, and is just one example of the variety of rain forest amphibians.

act responsibly in trying to develop rain forest areas. They encourage them to honor the United Nation's Convention on Biological Diversity, where nations are obliged to take action to protect its rarest species. Many indigenous people know that a balance is possible. People can inhabit and make a living from the rain forests without destroying them or the creatures that live there.

People all around the world are becoming more aware that creatures other than humans have a right to continue to exist on the planet. Reptiles and amphibians are not only part of the local ecosystem, but also part of the rich variety of life on Earth.

GLOSSARY

aquatic An animal or plant that lives in or near water.

bromeliads A group of plants that have a rosette of spiny leaves.

camouflaged When the shape, colors, or patterns of an animal help it to blend in with its surroundings.

canopy The layer of trees between the forest floor and the tallest towering treetops.

carnivorous Usually refers to an animal that feeds on the flesh or meat of other animals.

crustacean A hard-shelled animal such as a crab or lobster, which is usually aquatic.

decompose To rot, or to break down into component parts and chemicals.

ecological To do with the study of the inter-relationship between organisms and all aspects of their environment.

ecosystem The relationship of plants and living organisms to each other and to the environment.

ecotourism Helping to conserve rain forests by encouraging tourists to visit.

food chain A series of living things, each of which is dependent on the next for food.

fossils The remains of plants or animals from hundreds of thousands of years ago, preserved in solid rock.

hatchlings Young creatures that have just emerged from eggs.

herbivore Usually refers to a creature that eats only plants.

migration The seasonal movement of living things from one location to another.

nocturnal Describes a creature that is active mainly at night.

pesticides Chemicals used to control pests, such as flies.

pollutants Materials that harm the environment.

prehensile Part of an animal's body that can grab or act like a limb.

prey An animal that is hunted and killed by another for food.

species A group of plants or animals that closely resemble one another.

thyroid A gland in the neck that produces hormones that affect development.

wetland An area of land that remains waterlogged for most of the year.

White's tree frog.

FURTHER INFORMATION

Books to Read

Behler, John L. *National Audubon Society First Field Guide: Reptiles.* New York: Scholastic Trade, 1999.

Cassie, Brian. *National Audubon Society First Field Guide: Amphibians.* New York: Scholastic Trade, 1999.

Chinery, Michael. *Poisoners and Pretenders: Secrets of the Rain Forest.* New York: Crabtree Publishing, 2000.

Clarke, Barry. *Eyewitness: Amphibian.* Des Moines, IA: DK Publishing, 2000.

Deiters, Erica. *Animals of the Rain Forest: Tree Frogs.* New York: Raintree Steck-Vaughn Publishing, 2001.

Dollar, Sam. *Animals of the Rain Forest: Caimans.* New York: Raintree Steck-Vaughn Publishing, 2001.

Frost, Helen. *Rain Forest Animals: Boa Constrictors.* Minnetonka, MN: Pebble Books, 2002.

Steele, Christy. *Animals of the Rain Forest: Anacondas.* New York: Raintree Steck-Vaughn Publishing, 2001.

Young, Allen. *Tropical Rainforests: 230 Species in Full Color.* New York: Griffin Trade Paperback, 2001.

Video

National Geographic's Really Wild Animals: Totally Tropical Rainforest. National Geographic Video, 1994.

Organizations

Friends of the Earth
1025 Vermont Avenue, N.W., Suite 300
Washington, D.C. 20005-6303
Tel: 202-783-7400
Web site: www.foe.org

Greenpeace
702 H Street, N.W.
Washington, D.C. 20001
Tel: 1-800-326-0959
Web site: www.greenpeaceusa.org

Oxfam America
1112 16th Street, N.W., Suite 600
Washington, D.C. 20036
Tel: 202-496-1180
Web site: www.oxfamamerica.org

World Wildlife Fund
1250 24th Street, N.W.
Washington, D.C. 20037
Tel: 202-293-4800
Web site: www.worldwildlife.org

INDEX

caecilians 13, 15, 25
camouflage 18, 28, 31, 45
captive breeding 40, 44
chameleons 13, 16, 23, 25, 45
crocodilians 13, 19, 21, 44
  alligators 8, 13, 19, 27, 31
  caimans 5, 7, 10, 13, 19, 33, 35
    black 7, 32
    spectacled 7, 19
    yellow 7, 13, 26
  crocodiles 8, 13, 19, 22, 24, 27, 31, 43

dinosaurs 12

ecotourism 45
education 42, 43
eggs 7, 8, 9, 14, 34, 42

food chain 7
frogs 5, 7, 9, 13, 14, 21, 23, 24, 28, 31, 33, 34, 40, 43, 45
  African bullfrog 25
  banana 4
  bicolored tree 40, 41
  flying 31
  poison-arrow 5, 21, 28, 29
  pygmy marsupial 9
  smoky mountain 6, 34
  tree frogs 28, 40, 45
  White's tree 28, 33

hunting 7, 29, 35, 38, 41

iguanas 21, 27, 30, 33, 35
  green 16, 27, 28, 34, 35
  rhinoceros 27, 31

lizards (see also chameleons and iguanas) 7, 8, 10, 11, 13, 16, 21, 23, 24, 26, 27, 28, 29, 30, 31
  basilisk 16, 31

Chinese water dragon 33
  flying dragon 16
  fringed gecko 28
  Madagascan day gecko 16
  New Caledonian crested gecko 11
  sail-finned 12, 30
  skink 24
  tokay gecko 16
lowland forests 6, 20
  flooded forest 20, 41, 42
  mangrove forest 22, 42

medicines 40, 41
migrations 36, 37

newts 5, 8, 13, 15, 24, 29

pesticides 37
pet trade 33
poisons 14, 15, 26, 28, 29, 37, 40, 41
pollution 32, 36, 37, 44
predators 7, 14, 17, 19, 23, 24, 25, 26, 29, 30, 31
prey 5, 7, 14, 16, 17, 19, 22, 23, 24, 25, 26, 27

rain forest destruction 16, 32, 36, 38, 44
research 40

salamanders 8, 13, 15, 24, 29
  bromeliad 8
  tlaconete 15
skin 17, 30
  breathing through 15, 36, 37
  changing color of 11, 25, 28
  poisonous chemicals 14, 29
  shedding of 9, 30
  trade in 7, 34, 35, 35, 38, 39, 43

snakes 5, 7, 8, 10, 13, 17, 23, 24, 26, 27, 28, 29, 31, 34, 40, 41, 43
  African night adder 11
  anaconda 7, 9
  aquatic snake 21
  boa constrictor 17, 33, 35
  brahimy blind 17
  coral snake 17
  eyelash viper 26
  Madagascan tree boa 23
  mangrove pit viper 22
  red-tailed racer 5, 17
  sea snake 22
  spectacled cobra 32

tadpoles 8, 9, 21, 37
temperature 10, 11
toads 8, 14, 24, 28, 32, 41
  giant (cane) 14, 29
  golden 32
  goliath 14
tortoises 8, 13, 18, 21, 27, 28, 30, 32
tropical montane forests 6, 20, 23
turtles 8, 13, 18, 21, 27, 30, 36, 42
  Amazonian river 11, 18, 27, 34, 41
  axe 19
  green 22
  leatherback 19, 32, 37
  matamata 18

WWF 39, 43, 44